Other titles in the UWAP Poetry series (established 2016)

Keeper of
the Ritual

Shey Marque

Shey Marque was born in Perth, WA.
A former haematology and research
scientist, she has a Master of Arts in
creative writing and was Coordinator of
The Katharine Susannah Prichard Writers'
Centre where she currently coordinates the
Hospital Poets Program. Her award-winning
poetry has appeared in journals including
*Cordite Poetry Review, Meanjin, Overland,
Southerly, Westerly* and *Award Winning
Australian Writing.* Shey was the inaugural
recipient of the Queensland Poetry Festival's
Emerging Older Poet Mentorship Award in
2018. Her chapbook *Aporiac* was published
in 2016 with Finishing Line Press (USA).
Keeper of the Ritual, shortlisted in the 2017
Noel Rowe Poetry Award for an unpublished
manuscript, is her first full collection.

Shey Marque
Keeper of
the Ritual

Poetry

First published in 2019 by
UWA Publishing
Crawley, Western Australia 6009
www.uwap.uwa.edu.au

UWAP is an imprint of UWA Publishing
a division of The University of Western Australia

THE UNIVERSITY OF
WESTERN
AUSTRALIA

ISBN: 987-1-76080-023-9

A catalogue record for this
book is available from the
NATIONAL
LIBRARY   National Library of Australia
OF AUSTRALIA

Designed by Becky Chilcott, Chil3
Typeset in Lyon Text by Lasertype
Printed by McPherson's Printing Group

This project has been assisted by the Australian
Government through the Australia Council, its arts
funding and advisory body.

Australian Government

Australia
Council
for the Arts

 uwapublishing

MIX
Paper from
responsible sources
FSC   FSC® C001695
www.fsc.org

To John for bringing me here,
where the limestone slopes down to the sea

Contents

I

The remains of voice
　　　　　just a letting of air

Alligatorwood

Walk with me and I will show you sweet gums
where painted birds pummel us with trinkets
            like Caravaggio tossed artichokes
then I will push you backwards to her bark
coaxed to forget   with sap from early buds
        lulla lullaby   lulla lullaby

her *lu lu tong** will open your veins wide
        the scent of crab-apple and ambergris
and many autumn hands   settle on skin.
There's something of Judith about the scene
impressions of a woman passing by
            only moments ago   perfume hanging

        alongside the dried beds of a river
seed heads on stalks   and you caught by the hair.

* *Lu lu tong - Chinese herb from the fruit of a Liquidambar/American Sweet Gum (Alligatorwood)*

Flare-ups and Diminishings

i

The loss of sand is seen as an increase
      in view of ocean
through saltbush and scrub wattle
                    that lean over too far

they never quite make it back upright
      once the wind changes direction
in the way of hair as it carries winter salt
             turns over on itself

after facing into the gale   another tussock
beach spinifex with their heads full of seed
      uprooted
after last night's storm   and in the morning

how it takes no time at all to reach
the top of the dune   the soft slip over the edge
      loudly at first
our seagrass heads squealing

ii
No it doesn't take long
for the sun to set to fading   dead things
      weed and wood and cuttlefish bone
      hairstreak butterfly

how the grown-out highlights in her hair
                shine pale as chitin on the ragged wing
all structure of coil and dimension
breaking down to linear white

             in frequency of straight lines
we lie belly down on the sand
our curves covered with shell grit   and oil
mantis shrimp might see us turning

      emerald or blue
          or something altogether new
bright like *angspruchtenrose*
we couldn't begin to know this colour

Unpicking a Bird

To follow the wing of a herring gull
      is a meditation on balance

an invisible string links lead weight to scale
feather to foot   to my eye

the gull hops on one leg leans to the right
      extends a wing but doesn't fly

beak humbled on breast on clawed toe
on sand and rock   on my left forefinger

     fishing hooks catch on everything

Wind and waves bring onto the fringing reef
      every tangled and tethered

strangled thing   dead-eyed   belly up
the beach is a white-washed tomb

beautiful on the outside   on the inside
     full of bones of the dead   and the hobbled

bird   throat narrowed by nylon   a fisherman's
careless catch

falls limp on the grass   like an old toy
     fashioned from a white feather boa

and I am the puppeteer   unpack every wire
        every string   trying to make him dance

In the theatre of time-on-sky

The afternoon sun leaves rufous rags
      fallstreaks folding and unfolding
            deft like wanderers riding on the ship's sail
there's a woman giving an impromptu jig
mouth held just so   the lips
        still seem to open and close
the remains of voice just a letting of air
if I lean on the rigging   a beat
      has me dancing in the way of a dockside gypsy

she does a sideways step in red shoes
      not built for climbing
thumb and fingers taught to click   thread beads
      not touch the ropes that lift the mainsail
         cinnabar moth to the mast
beckoning from up there
her tin bangle falling to the deck
I reach forward to pick it up   straight-kneed
          extending a leg behind

to the waves' applause
her embroidered skirt gathers up the wind
      a couple of seabirds wheeling in the eddy
        my curiosity flung open
          tiny bells tintinning
then in the random way of buskers
      she disappears into rescinding light
the birds fall to rest
inspect the contents of their nest for bread

Patternicity

On a beach track at Two Rocks, a stone;
    its lime weighs down the sudden
minute. I watch sand swarm like bees

    that I once saw in a market town.
They sent people running into buildings
    for keys to lock their windows,

some woman with a goose was saying
    just because they're stripy
doesn't mean they are robbers. Honey

    bees covered the back of my shirt,
tangled in my hair, me not seeing much
    caught in that apoidean storm.

Still the sand spirals against my legs,
    its rough manner of being
stings me into knowing again that cut

    grass from the old lawn mower
spitting at me as it passed beside the path
    chalked in squares and numbers.

Now the swarming grit stops mid flight
    a thousand little engines stalling
at my feet. A specimen of limestone rock

its interior carved out like a hive,
the walls lined with tiny cavities, a nest
abandoned, as if the sand had wings.

Someone's Lost Sock

I've heard it said this is just an illusion—
the way a certain object (once noticed)
seems to reappear at a frequency too uncanny
for happenstance.

Soon you expect to see it everywhere
like you'd seek comfort or affirmation—
how an odd sock and its name
could hold some other meaning.

When he photographed it on the road,
that grey sports weave, I thought
its shape resembled a capital letter—
a beginning for loss, and love

he hid it, and he hid it

and it would keep turning up—
stuffed in a pocket of my jeans,
or an empty butter tub in the fridge, at the bottom
of my backpack after walking alone for days

and when I phoned late one night, he cut short
on the word *chaussette,* as if
it were caught in his throat,
as if it were something small

Children of Letters

Hazy is the humid Rockingham air
     and as we spell it out on the beach
no-one remembers the vowel liberated

     cart-wheeling over the sand
seaweed draws a line on the page
     so we can write the haze with bodies

and as we spell it out on the beach
     no-one remembers the vowel liberated
cart-wheeling over the sand

Handstand

Long after the tide has cleared those footprints from the beach
I stand at the edge of a picture
      watch your fingers take root
            in weathered castings of cuttlefish and shell
dunes behind me, now laced with wild weeds
your humid salt on the wind, on whitecaps, on my tongue.

Sinking through the emulsion, I stumble back to you
share your upside side view of the west, let loose
      change fall from my pocket, hear its soft thud to earth.
Fine sands lift across the shadows of clouds,
a chain bearing your name tumbles from my neck;
      glint of the key to your cottage on the hill.

I wink, whisper behind my hand
that secret hiding place among the Bougainvillea.

After Moving to the Coast

The shape of us shifted
for all I could tell
we were blue-eyed Selkies
        wailing low and long
salt-strong
colour of the night sea
dark-maned and muscled.

The moon turned a blind eye
that night   we disappeared
below the surface to dance
when we came
                back up for breath
you licked at the ocean
        as it rolled
                from my cheek
I couldn't tell if I cried.

How far away they seemed
        those city lights searching
a sky winking.

On the beach
miniature sand crabs
watched on   bug-eyed
waiting to collect
our shedding skins.

Close to Flying

Like stepping from the land into another gravity,
shifts in dexterity happen in the water. You keep
a tight hold on the rope to his halter, loop it, think

of the man who watched his horse swim away
in a straight line out to sea, nose up, no turning
ground, no way to bend him around. Yet still

you float over his back when the sandy floor falls
away and he's swimming. Both of you weightless,
it's skin to skin, breath to breath. Slide in, crouch

at his shoulder, feel the muscles work, his chest
expand beneath your bare feet, his breath quicken.
In clear water, diagonal pairs of legs in unison,

each hoof a paddle, the timing mechanical, hocks
and knees higher than a ground trot, head carriage
elevated and extended; it's underwater dressage.

Coming out of the sea, his whole body shakes, you
cling in stitches, nerves arcing with vibration, the fast
pull of the earth. In water there is never any falling.

The Settling of Wrecks

Folk here are of salt and lime, one eye always drawn to water.
If they turn away too long they won't notice traps set by the sea
and Two Rocks beach can be lavish with treachery and strays.

Few symbols to name such a place. Two pillars of limestone
by the groin. That there weren't a couple of dogs mating on the beach
that day is fortunate enough. Pointers to the wrecks. It's just the spot

to catch a wave or whiting, herring and blowfish (in my hands,
reverse that order). Seaweed festers on dog beach. Fumes
from boat and four-wheel-drive fuel mist the air at the marina.

Our community is boat-shoed and thonged. Neptune still rules
the town, its grocer pushes trolley trains, a baker chain smokes
in the sun, the almost homeless in apartments above cast out

prophecies from their balconies. Village street signs will remember
only yachts—America's Cup challengers from two centuries.
Dame Pattie and Gretel retire gracefully alongside Sappho, Valkyrie

and other fast women long since fallen into disrepair. We have cribbed
our beaches from the wishing well where a trail of guilders and myriad
old coins once littered the sea beds. In this museum without walls,

wrecks exhibit on reef and seagrass meadow. We rest on fretted dunes,
consider the demise of the sun, lick crusted salt from cuts and too many
margaritas, retell anecdotes about previous marriages and other ruins.

a day breaks in two rocks

blue is the shipping beacon, the scythe
in the sky, the exposed roots of yachts, the
squeak of drying, the spinifex skipping. blue
is monday morning. blue is two buoys squat-
ting, the ropes on their necks, the ears on the
sand, the crab holes winking, the large bowel
of beach. blue is monday morning. blue is the
last spit of summer, cray boats in arms, the
mussels clinging beneath, the forgotten gate
propped open, the no-swimming sign. blue is
monday morning. blue is the sanskrit sea, the
echo of a father's voice, two canvas shoes
parked on the jetty, a kiss on the sea bed, the
police light flashing. blue is monday morning.

The Changing Skin of Drowning

He had too many that last time   he left us
                        with six live ones
                a catch that was thorny sweet

Today the sirens are quiet. Paul doesn't hear them coming
                for him. Veiled in salt cloud
he and a buddy collect Western Rockies from their pot, its rope
                a scribble   winds a knot of the Gordian kind
around his ankle. Undone   shouting bubbles
fists snatching water   a knife falls.

His buddy never catches another cray but returns to the reef
                stares out at the rip current   again and again
lungs catch on a pang he mistakes for empathy
or adage
                because we really aren't fishes
and for five months carries a fisherman's words
                dive today and tomorrow I will dress in black.

Walking down the wooden stairway to the sand   for weeks
people are drawn to posies tied with spear grass to the handrail
                blue butterflies hover over saltbush.

Sometimes at night   a butterfly of blood red   swells
                inside the buddy's chest   grown so
that no manner of coughing can work it loose.
He thinks of invisible things like Paul
                crocidolite   friable filaments on the wind
snacks on apricot kernels and berries
                shallow breathes from his hospital mask.

The day he too drowns in air
neighbours gather on a balcony overlooking the sea   drinking
    drinking in the symmetry   in the doubling habit of fate
I notice the street heavy with wild rosemary
its bloom of bruise
        colour of storm cloud   relentless sea
        and that reckless earth of Wittenoom.

The Tweening

Her bones lie damp where they point to the wreck   beckoning
        to the ghosts of sailors   to the fallen   and the unwary.
She sifts through skeletons in her cellar beneath the sea   mementos
        to help her keep track of time and travellers past.
She layers seconds into eras and preserves them in brine   shakes them up
        to watch them fall again glitter in her water dome.

The sinklings tell of a lost Atlantis   and the beasts of arcady that drowned
        in the end unable to bear the sky.   Once dolphins
filliped within her belly   common as herring somersaulting   and bird men
        rallying   all wing and feather on those summer days
a headier century   days when we still believed we could fly.   Back then
        birth and death were carved in stone   all bound to salt and dust of lime.

A chain of vertebrae   hollowed and scoliosed with age   anchors her
        wetlands to the underworld   melds fiction to the real.
Miniature shrimp scamper against her hipbones   shelter in unbuttoned pockets
        bat wings tickle her sinuses   blind to the notion of loss
mosquito fish coalesce in codes foreign to her   over her head
        wild turkeys comb a parting through bulrushes   looking for seasons of rain.

Reveries pour from her cavernous mouth. Doorda Mia yawns   the resting place
        where wild dogs sleep. Dreams leak paint   into her lakes
water colours stream into wetlands where she washes   stories from brushes
        unfold on the banks of Pipidinny. Underwater tweening   silent evolution
inertia of unstill life   sea people transform a civilisation from antiquity
        to fantasy and fable   a Sun City   with a rock in place of a king.

In a Wood Wind

By the light of a pencil torch I practised
on my bed, head hung over the side,
goggles on and breathing through a flute,
hair floating buoyant as if really in the sea.

I'd loop a cord, throw it under the bed,
ease it over the plastic flask filled with brine,
tighten and haul in my wobbling catch with
the hint of a cray squeaking inside that bottled sea.

November the sea floor was littered with old skins,
trail of hollowed pell, leading out to deep water
and sea bananas gathered on the surface. We'd watch
pink-skinned 'whites' walking on to Rottnest.

There was a eucalypt wind that first time I fell
seal-black and finned over the side of the boat.
I took a fist of flute and stocking, limpets in the toe,
a stone to sink it into a hole in the reef.

Underwater I squealed out some tunes
while we hovered spider-like for the moment,
a cray's ragged claw would snag in the nylon weave
and sometimes on the webbing between fingers.

We didn't use pots anymore with fish heads
set on the seaward side of the reef. We learned
if occies or sealice didn't nick your bait,
thieves crept in late at night from out of town.

Back in the boat he said 'you know in the eighties
they put seal in their pots—or roo tail—
it sent the crays into a frenzy. Today
no-one'd admit it o'course—*no feathers or fur.*'

He said 'sometimes when the water's still
you can hear the fish laughing—*listen.*'
Under water I always found laughter
indistinguishable from a scream.

Feather Songs

i

A moon-walking bird struts backwards on a limb
singing through feathers, a pair of miniature violins
built into his wings. Tick tick *ting*, he plays

clubbed plume against shaft of seven nodes
with the unaffected air of a child virtuoso,
a solo riff on the world's first Stradivarius.

Pizzicato resonant in the hollow chamber, fatted quill
fingernail, hair or reptilian scale for *rachis* and *calamus*
and from his bones a thirty thousand year old flute

first instrument tuned on a wishbone. Only natural,
percussion becomes applause becomes a critic, tut tut
tutti of castanet moth and mini-cricket in the garden.

You set up a thousand vibrations under the skin
the fine sticking and slipping of bow across string
shimmer-itch in the forefinger, hum in the voice box.

Something in your code gives the voice of a bird
a vestigial tingling in the shoulder, a scar
it wants to stretch open, it wants to make noise.

ii

Outside my open window a white dove calls and calls insistent
        that he would have my violin to his nest.

Hear him ask for it in love-death notes from Wagner, this minim
        bleeding accidentals as he squats upon my sill.

Over the balustrade he throws each harmonic to its tiny death
        and I can't tell whether it's his note or mine, he

caught in mimicry, or if it is I who learn the song from him
        beckoning on a whim with bow outstretched so that

he may perch upon a powdered string, help me bring
        this trojan bird beneath my chin to tears. The release

of sound comes from some fiction of me; the white bird feathers
        my white lie, waits for the seeds I offer then leaves.

Juniper

My mother she killed me, my father he ate me, my sister she gathered all my bones,
tied them in a silken scarf, laid them beneath the juniper tree, tweet tweet...
Jacob Grimm

It's not from an absence of mothering
                    this fear of being devoured
                            of being swallowed whole
        but from a doubling
                and the mere possibility of exchange

            Sheltered in the canopy   a large soft hand
                    naïveté sits eating an apple
                    and there is release
        back on the ground   a shifting of the plane

        Looking over one shoulder, strange tracks
                        instead of shoes   three toes
                the two-footed hopping
                        fools no one in the end   blue-
        purple petals hanging from the mouth of a wren

                            twigs from twisted bough clenched
        with cuckoo fruit between white teeth,
                and a song at once beautiful and sad so sad
        hop

        It wouldn't be the first time
                            that I should lose
                    my head over a dangerous berry
        hop hop

And that box
of ashes still on the bookshelf
they haven't gotten around to scattering them yet
nor buried any bones in the garden

There's a marble hidden inside the bowl of keys
that one with the black pivot eye
for a sister type who may first hold then plant me in the spring
hop hop hop

White scarf that once hid my ruptured neck hangs
on the back of a chair
folded in a way
so as to know the child that I was
red as rose and white as snow
hop hop

And a stone of lime cleaved from the hilltop
if one stands too close to the edge
would take away the pedestal
of a mother type
should she don her brown coat and overstep
the whole thing falls
hop

I find my head
sleep emerges from its shadow
seeps into the skin of the Juniper tree
becoming creaturely
with gravity and wind

until old bones protrude through follicles
in the hillside
I barely know my own hands
starveling fingers drop a blue-black spice
and I can see now it's inevitable
despite some bitter moments   I am and have always
been edible

A Family History

for Anne

I'm sorry I hid your banana and strung it
up on the ceiling that day in the staff room
when you left to answer the telephone.

I swapped it for an old skin of mine
to make you think you'd already eaten it
but I left and didn't get to see your face.

No-one warned me about your memory, and
your silence I mistook for indifference when
you were just afraid to say the word out loud.

Woman in the Waters of Lethe

Deny you feel the end's menacing gaze
glide with the Manta ray, breast against spine
brace yourself beneath the tumbling waves

Wipe salted lashes and wrap them in swathe
swim blind across the oblivion line
deny you feel the end's menacing gaze

It's over—these words you squeeze and rephrase
as if that will change the meaning behind
brace yourself beneath the tumbling waves

Enticed by the fleuve, in drunken fantase
your eye cast adrift from the warning signs
deny you feel the end's menacing gaze

Loose tendril of truth enmeshed in brocade
old memory hermits crouched in the mind
brace yourself beneath the tumbling waves

Across intuition your sacred trait
grows monogamous femme's security vine
deny you feel the end's menacing gaze
brace yourself beneath the tumbling waves

Nude Descending a Staircase

If ever I were to put my hand to clay, take a knife to stone or dip a mould
into molten bronze, it would be to summon into being this image in anaglyph
from a time when I viewed you as art. Contour of you frozen in single mom-

ents, a series of still frames under single phase lighting of the stair well. Your
walk suspended in mid air. Strobing in the night you are a film star reborn from
a bygone era featuring in an old black and white home movie. Stepping down

through the dark, robe cast in flight behind your right shoulder, the weight on
your back foot, three fingers pinning the hair from your face. But what feat-
ures would speak of sleepiness, complete unawareness of being watched and

preoccupation of events from a nascent dream that leaves behind a smile which
crumples when you catch sight of me standing there in silence, holding my
breath, waiting for you to fall awake? You demand to know why I lurk so late

scheme to frighten, leave crumbs in your bed. I touch your hand and lie to you
promise never to do it again, tell you it is me who raids the refrigerator, makes
the mess in the kitchen during the night. Much later you take those stairs, skin

weathered like sandstone in the wind, somehow rendered more precious with time
textured to the touch, a kinetic effigy. Only this time when you reach me you
don't stop humming Bellini's haunting melody from *La Sonnambula*. Ballerina

you just float on by in *bel canto*. I wish I could recall the song's title however
the name eludes me as many names do. Something in me of you. I wonder aloud
whether your exposed skin is cold but no response of the verbal kind. Red scarf

hangs on the coat rack, winds its woollen way around your neck a split second before the front door closes. I find I have become Balanchine's poet, hesitant to wake you into ignominy, yet afraid not to should you plummet from sleep.

So I shadow you in *pas de deux*, try to catch the rhythm of your whispering feet fathom the purpose in those eyes that glisten beneath their mask of glass, feel the weight in your arms as I manoeuvre you back before the final act is sung.

Early this morning I open my eyes, brush away the white salt and pine needles to find bruises on both shins, my clothes scattered over the wooden steps above the sea. Gentle waves roll in, your effigy of sand melting in the foam.

You Over There

Just tell me what you did today
if only to keep a tiny piece of you in my day
and a bit of me in yours. Ten years of distance
crammed into this email, two sentences
pretend you haven't much to tell. You used to say
our paths ran in parallel. My life could be yours
in as much as yours could be mine.
A neighbour once mistook your knees
for my knees, said that meant we were sisters
or maybe cousins. I never could recognise
the curve of my own profile, the shape of my laugh,
the vocabulary of my walk. Tell me what you see
when you think of me, if ever you do,
if you can still remember how
to help remind me who I am on the outside,
what the back of my hair really looks like.

Last Words

I keep reading it over and over; a paper thing folded and then unfolded. Each time
the form of you changes like a tricky piece of origami. Maybe it's just the chaos
of a waking mind and the pages nothing more than the wing of a hand-made glider.

Some words can take on odd meanings and if looked at long enough
the point comes where they seem untenanted, the sentiment they once held gone,
fled back inside the hand that wrote them. Still I lay it face up on the grass,

imagine someone has stood on a mountain, thrown paper horses skyward
and if you make like a weary traveller they'll find you, transform to flesh and blood,
carry you back. But they're more like birds; transient and too fragile to bear weight.

How tense is the sudden potential of voice as I read your letter out loud;
its strange physicality. The winter's day makes mists of words, the shape of them
solid in the air, as if the mere sound of your name might cause you to manifest

—a lazy eyelid, ragged moustache, or wet light on gumnut and ironbark.

II

As the moment releases itself from the weight of scale...

Chasing Cello Joe

at the coda jazz supper club   san francisco
    he runs away with bach's little fugue

soughing to the fretless curve of hip and cello
    and a man's talking fingers
we haven't a thing to do in the moment
         except pine   yes we do that with finesse
and we dance our own vernacular
me meaning to catch   you falling anyway

it's the eclipse festival   palmer river
    his strings are powered by a bike girl

standing before the sun in that way
you are a cut-out   a blackened keyhole
       a thing abandoned or missing
like when the moon takes a bite of the sun
    throws a casual pall upon the earth
by the angle of your chin   I can tell you're gone again

and what of the weird gesturing
    with his fingers backlit as they move?

there is a brightness to their periphery
that strange script   a hybrid indefinable
    like the unit of us
leaving the vic night market its gutter full of apples
       bin of withered lettuce
me cycling ahead   you lagging behind

The Fetishist Listener

it's in the clutter of bows   the fingers plucking
     the counting with feet   nodding of heads
couples dancing
     the nonchalant cigarette   the sigh in the sax
this feeling trapped in amber

not accessible in any other way
     but with the first few bites of the phrase
     like Proust's little cakes dipped in tea
an old movie starts playing
handful of sweet midnights   the blue ones
     when she went upside your head
I went up to the rooftop to hum

again on the walk home from the beach
     I can smell seaweed air   saltwater hair
         and coconut
feel the bamboo mat beneath my feet
     in that small rented apartment
     counting the steps as I dance to that song
a gradual ripening of sunburn   on my shoulders
     on my cheeks   that first time you made me say
         I love you

With a Naked Eye

Midday on a Sunday
  semester break 1992
I'm outside at Gino's
on the cafe strip in Freo
composing a headache
  out of espresso
  and a jazz trumpet.

Sitting near the roadside
each with our hypotheses
  on the table
each in competition
  with the traffic
jumping
at the occasional car horn
and the maître d's voice
  close enough to my ear
  to feel the hair
  on his vocal chords.

We do the student thing
dine on the yeast
  of pizza and beer
and this is the day
I discover green olives
  and blue cheese
approaches the ketonic
taste of squashed ants.

We share the gorgonzola
all ear fuzz and old cobweb
        its junk
        an accidental hero
like the physician
who eats s-shaped bacteria
        to get himself an ulcer
        maybe a Nobel Prize.

As the moment releases itself
        from the weight of scale
the sky reveals
spores of grey-green cloud
birds infecting the air
        multiplying their small m's
        to vanishing point.

Abstract of a PhD in verse

Attempting to tease out dystrophic theories,
eg; the discontinuous from the continuous,
I confess I found functional domains testing.

By that I mean their E-box, basic tails and
leucine zippers sent me for a helix-loop-helix,
both of us at once loving and repelling water.

They had a history of being reserved and stable
unless you disrupted their composure. Odd that
those who came before found them in a fruit fly

; they were *hairy* and *daughterless*. We talked
incessantly of destroying and building muscle,
alternated between cell death and regeneration

used code words that began mostly with m.
Turns out most of those allelic variants were
neither sufficient nor necessary for success,

although by chance you could use some of them
to tell certain mice apart from one another.
On balance, it's all a matter of intermediates

; whether or not they are present. We thought
it best to put the spotlight on a gang of minors,
the ones that never act alone, no-one to blame.

A Geranium Grows in the Wall

I'm not a decipherer of auditory things
for instance   I can't tell rain
        falling on a tin roof   from applause
the spit of aspirin or the shifting of sand
        like time chafing out a wormhole
and the memory of sound   an infidel
so I trace contour with forefinger
focus on space and air between
        listen with eyes   to find
                the things that might be heard there

No I'm not a decipherer of auditory things
in this house   her word protests without breath
a struggle grows from moss and lime
puts on lipstick and rouge
        stands on the verandah
                waiting for you to pass by
the red on green after-image hangs
        lacquered toothy grin
        webbed hands waving

If only I were a decipherer of auditory things
I could recover
        sound from minute trembling
                (like conversation from a potato chip bag
                        or a glass of water)
map leaf movement to frequency
                petal to harmonic

because it seems to me
the geranium might be delivering
     poems from *The Earth Lover*
     soliloquy for a Russian   or a husband

Foal Watch

Once the waxing and bagging is done
    there's pawing and the slow piaffe

the sweet smell of fresh hay on the floor
    her tail woven to a thick braid.

The storm in the trees creates a new sky
    reverses the pattern of lamp light

scattered in the stable, blue-lit fragments
    borrowed from a cubist moon.

It's the standing position that surprises
    when two small hooves appear

then in one ocean-like movement, a wave
    of baby is spilled from the mare

its slippery pod caught by a foal watcher
    peeled open. To a slant eye

this colt could be a will-o'-the-wisp,
    a lightning sprite, or a min min

he could be all of these things or nothing
    but the notional bending of light.

Transience

'Youth at Broome', Russell Drysdale, 1958

This terracotta statue of a boy has walked
from the kiln of wood-fire sky, clay-baked earth,
and the day has cast him sweating with reds

String of tin pearls strewn on the horizon
separates him from the teeming sea, and
the settlement only looks whiter from here

His identity is made slippery by snake
or hat shadow, shirt the colour of Chinatown,
legs absorbed back into the shifting sand

I want to cup both hands around my mouth
scream *look behind you*, as a car wreck
twists into the air and slithers above him

Chicanery of light on the air lavish with dust
changes the shape of things, on second glance
he is both harlequin and phantom of the desert,

having only a brief encounter with form
morphing like an old world lizard, flicker,
a loose connection before my unhinged eye

The Light Painter

'The Blue Hour' by David Gilliver

To me, light painting is an expression of our true selves.
It's about the trace we leave behind
Patrick Rochon

Light is nothing until it touches something. Human-
ity is a blinking bulb. The porch lantern is always on
sensor. Popp's thought bubbles of vibration, imagin-
ation, sound, emotion, from helices flashing in code.

But what of the shape of a sound, the texture of feel-
ing, the colour of thought? I think in a series of aqua
rings. Painted over the midnight canvas behind eye-
lids lie minute tinted spots. Closer and closer to me

they come – I know they are near since they are get-
ting larger – throbbing with growth then retract again
mimic the dynamics of a lava lamp. My orbs dwell-
ing inside, symbiosing every thought, transforming

each into light. Soft as the touch of moonlight, ball-
ooning spheres like amnion wait to engulf my body.
I climb in and roll, spinning on the skin of a mount-
ain lake. By the seaside, I am the nucleus of medusa

crystal jellyfish. Globe riding, sphering, zorbing, hill-
rolling. I have become the orb. Encapsuled, luminous
myriad loops of chartreuse and emerald on this even-
ing's ebbing tide, reflecting to malachite and back.

Storm on the Swan

Storm on the Swan by Elise Blumann, Art Gallery of Western Australia

I wondered if the trees knew a storm was coming
leaves turned upward to catch the falling rain.
Or did they purge the river through their veins
then make it rain by way of humble dance?

Such a storm blurs all boundaries, the river
as if a sea. Air and water become one, an alloy
on my breath, on my tongue, become one
with the earth and the shadows of trees

limbs forced horizontal in the slipstream
paddle naked in the rain, the weather
posing brazen before the artist's eye
has settled into character for the day.

Tilt your head. Does the sky resemble the river
or the river the sky? Either way
this is the type of rain you can smell coming
on a humid day, on a day like this

I raise my head to search scud clouds
remember a time in Lajamanu
when the sky and the river changed places
picture that swarm of spangled perch

as they fell from the sky, their forked tails,
pectoral fins useless to paddle in air.
Somewhere, I thought, there must be a cat
rubbing a pearl shell, performing a rain dance.

Settina for Juliette

Before there was the river
I knew a green canvas, thread
onto steel poles, filled with hose
water tasting of metal
and dead ants, and a current
was a whirlpool in the bath
after pulling out the plug.

I understood its power
from the suction on my thigh
resting too close to the drain.
When we moved to the Canning
it was the start of swimming
lessons, and the first I learned
of drowning, a girl like me.

I heard she got stuck in mud,
in the way of dumb cattle
caught in a flood, no sense of
self-preservation, they said.
I thought I saw her pale hand
on leaving that wooden plank
to duck dive in deep water.

It was mirror, then filter,
a distorted lens, bent light,
and I felt the magician's
easy hands separate me

from the bottom half of my
orange bikini, its frill
floating off just out of reach.

As it sank, I could've sworn
there was a subtle pulling.
While I shook on the jetty
wrapped up in my dad's towel,
again I thought I saw her
features limpid and dripping,
much closer this time, one eye

reflecting sun, the other
a spiral. Look, he said, how
many faces you can see
in the churning. They're not
real, just as there are no dogs
within the knots and wood grain
on the old floorboards at home.

Yes I knew that was the place
where branches had died and fell
and the circling was a scar.
There was no end to circles,
their beginnings forgotten
like those limbs were never there
waving for help as they went.

Friday in the City

Only time gives this breeze its name.
Even the air has lost its way, bent
around corners of buildings, diverted
down back alleys. In such a wind you fly
your freak flag like a home-made kite.

The day passes without direction, no
hint of horizon or which way is north.
At night, south is only a calculation,
its crux invisible beneath white noise
of street lamps, headlights and neon.

You wear the chaos like a middle name
inherited from that eccentric aunt,
feel the pull of thread while it knits a cat-
collecting gene into your DNA. As you walk
by an op shop your swivel eye is drawn

to a red beret and purple scarf. You worry
it won't be long before you start drinking
your first martini before noon, and dance
barefoot without music in the street
that day when words are just another noise.

On an Empty Day

Let me hold in my hand this novel in soft cover. It smells
      like a pine cupboard
the kind in which you never store wine glasses. I imagine
      the story is a new merlot
all berry and cheek, the one you choose when you need
      some light-hearted tale
to wind down from stories of suicide and refugee camps.
      Give me bitch wine
for its chick lit in a bottle, all pink bows and patchwork stitching
      all hearts and lipstick label.
Bend me some dog ears and let me sip without a glass,
      leave my stain on every page.

Another Wasted Day

Killing time with cheap red wine
      some bottle incapable of aging.
First light I woke with a nosebleed
      the bittersweet brightened me
white as meringue, pink like chilli lipstick
      the dry eye of morning is upon me.

Untold years have hurtled to the wire.
      If there were prints, I never saw them
no tracks pressed into the earth.
      They have washed everything white.
In the late morning sun I watch
      my form fading, dog chasing the shadow.

Notes on a Bulgarian Music Teacher

He speaks inside your bones with his past,
haemorrhage of bruised sea on the beach.

Irises, soft and violet, drift back to the war, he
spindle tall as if a flower in the cupboard.

Milk in the soup bubbles over, he says, *and
the burn will leave a slippery cicatrice on your tongue.*

You lay awake on the night of the lost sleep
gleaning for the lesson in his tone.

Insomnia increases life by one third
so he works amid the immortality of darkness.

Through the telescope he sees tranquillity, a place where
everything is round, sharp edges gone.

Last night I saw him sitting on a hilltop, gazing at Jupiter,
reciting poems of silk and cyanide.

He said he was happy.

Only the Music

I teased him a lot that summer
played flat notes in all the wrong places
tuned my own tongue to mimic his
           Baltic inflections
told him that I thought
      con brio means with cheese
             just to see his eyes widen
said how fine it was for him
to have all day to devote to music
        now he was retired.

By day I worked in haematology
trading afternoon shifts and penalty rates
      for evenings at the cello.

Midnight to dawn shift was the hardest to swap
liver transplants had only just begun
      all night in theatre they bled and bled
I matched type with type A or B
packed blood in shuttle canisters
sent them into orbit through the hospital arteries.

During the lull at three in the morning
I slumped in the staff room and drank
      coffee to keep me awake through hump hour
thought about cello practice and this
regular excuse for not doing any

to be expressed with downcast eyes
        ten thumbs and a sigh
            the next day.
He half listened to my unimproved piece
        Vivaldi's second Sonata in F major

while he spoke of a past career
student at the conservatorium by day
cosmic physicist by night.
I stopped playing to ask when he slept
     half hour here
          twenty minutes there
not many about in the small hours.
You and I, he said
we need not be so different.

In a small town in Michigan

you see me once the music starts
move back to where I never was
turning into a swing kitten
it's impossible to keep still

and I'm dancing to Glenn Miller
in the streets of war-torn Paris
the time before he was a spy
stolen from a brothel by rogues

eyes closed and I'm singing that
I got a gal in Kalamazoo
in a t-shirt that says yes
there really is a Kalamazoo

Leonard Cohen's Writing Room

Your old axe on the wall to the left of a glass pane
would snatch songs as they float in on the late air.

There's a song you wrote I can't bear. It lures me
to thoughts of self hate let in on the sly by a soft tune.

Words still rest on the straw plait seat of the chair,
in the warp and weft of the scrap bin, and the beats

come in sine waves in the sheet on the day bed
where the sweat of sweet fools clings to their weave.

Out in the yard I can't tell if the bloom is mauve
just as you could not see why your arm was not a tree.

Your book was born in the midst of rocks and weeds,
lent to me by a red haired guy I've not seen

for twelve years now. He called it a strange mix
of jazz riffs, pop art jokes and slant views of sex.

But it turns out he was just one more wreck
who wants to steal your words and pimp your style.

With my eye turned now from the lost and the rot
to seek some place where the streets are spare

I will think of you in the key that rusts, a loose quill,
up in the third-floor room of that white stone house.

Like the Finch

I don't mind the quiet in a nest
can learn to like solitude   think of it as the distance between notes
        and in reverse the same can be said
insert melody into silence   singing in this cage of ribs
    only   your long absences are harder to fill
        with excuses or the song of finches.

To the silence of infinity   we walk at right angles
    toward a landscape so set in reverse
even music cannot find its way
        to carve such absence on trees   in which finches hang
          upside down and mute from branches
        ring barked   by desire for larger fruit.

Curves are all that is left over   the reverse of a letter I
    carved your absence into yesterday's ghost gum
sensuality of torso   stroked by finch feather
    silence grafted onto my own body
        like the bean that swells inside
sweet twin   violin.

In reverse sense   you and I are near
    vena umbilicalis   *carry my blood to him*
we share pitch and rhythm
    listen to the Doppler (absence of silence)
        my little dog yaps to the galloping hoofs
        while finch wings flutter on rousing.

This frenzy of presence   rests in silence
unspoken   because my message
     if delivered by words becomes reversed
          creates only a string   of spongy symbols

          absence soaking up a certain view
asking to be taken the wrong way.

On the floor
     beside my writing desk
a finch's nest filled with paper eggs
     cracks in their shells
          there's scratching and writhing inside   silence is dying
spheres of doubt   hatching absence.

Tiny finch beaks open and close in silence

Stealing Strawberries

I am limbo dancer, I am jewel thief
replete with weave and flex, chicanery
becomes me, double-curved around the girl
as a python hugs an egg in the nest.

Placing my feet soundless in the garden
I crouch close to the ground in the torch glow
my bare hands unfurl red berries beating
there's a hint of Virgil's child of the earth

gathering wild fruit in the summer grass
unaware of the danger waiting near,
when in the dark of night, a sensor light,
the chill of someone standing over me,

my mouth full with strawberries, the stain
of all your broken hearts bleeding on my chin.

Me, Susan & Jacques Prévert

Tiens — laisse-moi prendre tes mains si froides

wait, I'll take your cold hands and we'll jog
down the avenues of Dijon, gloves dangling
and gesturing from our pockets, stumble on
chestnuts and chase every hair and feather

of the hoards squirreling away from the rime;
we'll slough our leaves of scarves and coats
in a café on the corner of a fountain, sipping
rose, pomegranate and pamplemousse tea;

we'll elasticise elusive verbs, stretch them
work the vowels over our tongues until midi;
capture a nuance between thumb and forefinger
whittle it to a point and pluck it free, then

we'll ride that carousel on the cobbled street
practise something simple like a poem
about how to paint a portrait of a bird and we
begin by leaving the cage door wide open.

Later we'll sit in the afternoon sun drinking
kir royale from plastic flutes with the geese
and wild boar in the park, all the while mistaking
phalluses for virgins, French letters for jam.

A Bowl of Lyre Birds

In the wake of my hunger the worm woke to find
an art form, its creature swimming. In my soup

bowl three painted lyre birds superb in cobalt and teal
chin down, tail up, one foot lifted as if an etching

peeled from the surface of a ten cent coin or one
hundred-dollar note left behind from diners passing.

In the distance I can hear the clattering of crockery,
a car alarm, a chainsaw. A camera shutter just

behind me. A kookaburra interrupts the city noise,
syrinx still flexing. The lyre birds copy their flavour

to my tongue, recall aroma of wild pheasant and guinea
fowl, recoil at the neighbour in detention. I'd rather

consume the lyre bird amid all its sass and backtalk,
its brass-necked poise, its life designed for levity,

than the chicken, missing her tail feathers, flavour
tainted by guilt, a life defined only by slaughter.

Plume

Femme qui Tire son Bas by Henri de Toulouse-Lautrec, 1894, oil on cardboard, 58 × 46cm, Musee d'Orsay, Paris

Flesh shimmers in the powder white
turquoise pours over shoulder lakes
black silk slides where sighs begin
mirage in the night of Toulouse-Lautrec

Turquoise pours over shoulder lakes
trace my contours in slow motion
mirage in the night of Toulouse-Lautrec
sense of me in the boudoir rouge

Trace my contours in slow motion
spin the threads from an artist's gaze
sense of me in the boudoir rouge
brushed paint peeled from a canvas past

Spin the threads from an artist's gaze
colour me back to another day
brushed paint peeled from a canvas past
a plume from Montmartre at my feet

Colour me back to another day
black silk slides where sighs begin
a plume from Montmartre at my feet
flesh shimmers in the powder white

Alice before Wonderland

Alice Liddell as 'The Beggar-Maid', Lewis Carroll, 1858

White dress ripped from one shoulder by hands
unmarked of earth, her left breast a new bud,

chichi shedding modesty under a cloud to wallow
ephemeral in sunlight. A sideways glance defies you

to ask, her palm a demitasse outstretched, begging
for grace but her face can't find a pattern for pain.

Hunger is just a name, a mere figure of pretence
barefoot in crumpled nasturtiums. Picture a waif

standing in a poem by Tennyson, trying on a skin,
Penelophon poised, waiting to catch the eye of a king.

Angel on a Bicycle

'Angel on a Bicycle', Czech Carnival in Olomouc, Josef Koudelka, 1968

Wings of cotton at rest, bell untouched, he is pedalling
an ordinary life, keeping pace alongside gypsy horses
marking time with hooves over cobble stone. Exposed

against a background quotidian, boy in white robe plays
silent as a pantomime in which purity is the cameo star
cast as a metaphor for exile. Even from this distance

the rumble of tanks can be felt through the main streets
of Prague. Old woman, hand on hip, watches hope and futility
share the stage as the two old friends become reacquainted.

Neruda's Sixteen Finches

It's difficult to see the glass ceiling because it's made of glass. Virtually invisible. What we need is for more birds to fly above it and shit all over it, so we can see it properly.

Caitlin Moran

Insanity and great affection go hand in hand. If your love is for *animalia* then this
is a sign that you will be judged (can it be?) It's only Hector Malot thinking
out loud inside your head. Not so loud! Neruda hears humming; a fragile mind is
more creative. I see her travel with sixteen finches and a violin or two no less
with a husband *or two*. All fit side by side on a rack. And her stance strong
not at all unladylike (she holds captive) all the wild beasts gather 'round her

(lucky charm) like Orpheus, sweetened by sixteen notes, oh brother! just for a lark
Neruda seeds an idea to be unshelled, tasted, spitting husks of insanity to finches
fine feathers not a sign that the bird can sing, *no humming please,* nor a fiddle
by name alone befickled of reputation. (I've overheard it said) only a man *or lesbian*
could stroke those curves, make it sing so (like a beast), make the maker redundant.
And behind his hand, hinted in the dark, *you know,* how she might as well

smoke enormous cigars, drink stout, play golf (insane I hear, a rodent humming)
rat-catching, fetching finches; teach them all that as well at sixteen years of age.
Watch how the world would play (believe) if not for Neruda or the great painters.
Hang the answer in les *Halles,* see the birdie (goldfinch) in the picture, look for the sign!
Bellini is there copying a feminine figure onto canvas; curves out of the frame
(read an artist's eye) a violin and a woman bleed together, a medieval beast mixed

from the same oil. No need for such humming gentlemen (we're English). Remember
that the beak holds no more (significance) than the feather. *Sshh* The picture speaks
(a beast) of grace, sixteen bunches of erase-me-nots. Even the devil's fiddler had
an answer; an insanity of sorts, his imitations of a donkey, a swatch of horse hair
this is the sign in defence of *she* who would not be silenced (insulted) not ignored.
And as for those finches perched high on a single string (to whom do they belong?)

Yes, the witches *will* dance on the grass underneath the walnut tree (despite) a hubbub
of howling, insane humming like tinnitus, a tribe of warriors *in your ear!* Give it time
you will see the sign (think back) how the fiddler fitted right into the crowd of sixteen
revellers (swooners); black of dress, of hair, of eye, of bird. The moment the beast
cries out *mad wicked folly,* liberates finches and ladies (Victoria is not amused).
One by one he creates a star in the midst, convenes a meeting of the weird sisters.

Sister do not consent to be sung only in the manner they wish (understand) you alone
can cause your wooden lung to sing it real. Listen to (Nicolo's) little bell, it's a beast
of kind reply, for this is the sign. Hear your goldfinch twitter at the tip of the steeple.
Strike the violin sixteen times in staccato, study in Italy (or France) call home any place
where the Master prizes talent above all humming. Stride forward through time;
insanity has a magnificent portal (with gilded cornices) and twelve foot mirrors.

I'll keep a fine bowing arm (fine beau on my arm), sixteen finches and a humming
bird, sign of a beast, and see my violin kissed by the fiddler as if an old Cremona
at auction. Delicious insanity! Witch be near me. Mirror me on the path of Neruda.

Keeper of the Ritual

In a rhythmic hand on page twenty-eight of her *journal intime*, third *arriére grandmére* records a violin lesson and this photo lures her to me; a state of hiraeth. Music lessons remind me of her. I could almost be her. Maybe I *am* her. I see her Parisian master pace the studio end to end, head erect, back straightened, jacket tails aflounce. A cane in his right hand taps the ground with every second stride. Arising from the sepia, his scrutiny of gaze on my corps impresses upon me *l'art du violon*.

Baillot's Posture bends me, pushes the weight onto my left side, right foot just touching the ground, lends to my right arm an arc unconstrained, freedom against the still anchor of my body. Form manoeuvres in a manner more becoming, places the right foot turned outward forty five degrees. Massart waves his cane in my direction, as if a wand, summons perfection. Momentarily the melody causes me to falter, *tomber en pâmoison,* and his frown shifts toward my right foot. Right on

cue, the master's stick fair cuts through air, and an old habit is banished from my stance. I am compelled to take off both shoes and practise arpeggios with *un oeuf du poule* placed beneath my bare right foot. These days so many raw eggs lie broken, yolk oozing through stocking to toe before she comes to reshape my awkward shadow. I feel those strings. It's a game we play to remain connected. Ceremonial. A trick of the cells. For I am nothing if not her code fragmented again and again.

III

For a moment the mantel clock ticks backwards

Harlequin Street

I run up the hill after gymnastics. On our front verge my bare legs
pas de chat, flecked with green confetti, catch a shower of grass.

Dad motors over the lawn and laughs. He doesn't notice my batman-
masked brother jump from the roof of the garage onto the strip of lawn

down the centre of our driveway. Emerging from the afternoon shade
my brother springs upright, kneecaps of green. Beside him

my sister fumbles a tape measure and chalk in her hands. Inside, Mum raps
against the lounge room window, wags a finger. Through the flyscreen, the house

smells like grass and cupcakes. I shake off my gym shoes at the door. Two open
bags of plaster of Paris lean on the fence, leaking chalk dust. My siblings' pale

faces grinning in the kitchen. The cat hisses, slinks by on her belly. Raw sausage
mince thaws on the sink, melts in my mouth. My slippery fingers plunge

into the chest freezer, sneak inside a plastic bag and pull out a fist of frozen
peas which tumble onto the tiles like a broken string of pearls. Unwinding,

feet up in front of the television and snifter beside him on the table, Dad
hollers at the umpire for having only one eye. He doesn't see Bradley outside

the boy next door who still toddles in a nappy that bangs on his knees. Bradley
slaps me and says fuck off. On the lawn his sister Lesley slides into the splits

arms extended either side, palms splayed, fingers twirl a flourish. I copy
her but get stuck half way. She waves to my mum, calls her 'aunty'. I shadow

her cartwheels around to her back door step. Inside, her mum wipes dry a glass
on her dressing gown. I wonder if I should call her mum 'aunty' but the word hides

under my breath. Bradley's mum blows smoke rings at the table while he climbs on her
lap. Down in their henhouse a single rooster crows. Their father's flushed face yawns.

On the cherry laminex an ashtray, potato chips, aspirin and rum. Bradley squeals,
his father gives him a Chinese burn and an open hand. I fall backwards into a bendback.

After dinner Lesley bangs on our door, says her mother won't wake. Dad tells her
to stay with us while he calls triple zero and runs next door. Mum feeds her spaghetti

and an ice-cream cone piled higher than mine. Outside, the red light of an ambulance
flashes while my family watches Roadrunner. I practise a pirouette and Lesley does

the splits until Bradley's mum comes home to collect her. Early in the morning, three
of them drive away and I wave goodbye. The station wagon is stuffed with pillows

and running shoes. I see the father's hooded face peering out of the front room window,
red and yellow diamond curtains draped around his body. Later he is frogmarching

down the driveway with two men in suits. Running out onto our front lawn, I perform
a trio of forward flips then stop and fall slowly back into a bendback, hanging there,

I think my face might explode. Next day, Lesley's family still haven't come home. Again my legs slide over the grass and stop short of the full splits. My brother and sister

imitate me, giggling. Beside the rubbish bin next door, empty bottles tinkle as they fall from green bags. Tea leaves from Mum's silver teapot cascade into the rose garden.

My family never goes anywhere.

The Sleepover Sonnets

i

Outside the house next door there's a tin
letterbox in deciduous orange
hanging from its post by a rusty bolt,
filled with a week's letters, corners eaten,
the envelopes covered in tiny shells.
There was never anything except bills
and brochures—junk mail was a novelty,
something the neighbourhood kids fought over
propped up on our elbows, legs sprawled
bare-skinned over the sculpted brown carpet
each bagsing one of the toys—the biggest
tugging and blustering through gritted teeth
in the way dogs fall into hierarchy
all show and uncomfortable surrender.

ii

We were mostly quiet during the day
while her mother had another migraine
and a silent flu that never ended
in her towelling dressing gown and slippers
cross-legged on a lime green kitchen chair
bottomless cup of tea on the table
her reflex faux frown when we whisper-shrieked
pointing out glossy pictures—the bargain
totem tennis, dragster and roller skates,
her monotonic *yairs yairs* a standard
quick wonky smile if she caught me looking
for too long at the pattern that had formed

on her face—darkened rings about her eyes
repeating blue over cheekbone and chin.

iii
I half changed into something else that night
while my friend was sleeping right along side
—I had become much more like a mollusc
soft bellied and clad with a thickening shell
like the white snail that devours the mail
retracting and recoiling to the touch
coming out again when the heat is gone—
and in the morning, ice cream and coffee
all the wrong things never allowed at home
so many scenes played out here were new
even from the inside of my sleeping
bag zip done up as far as it could go
there's the critter of her brother's fingers
still alive and laggard upon my chest.

Sometimes Behind the Wallpaper

Down in my grandmother's garden I slip
through the chicken-wire gate that leads to the stone
steps of the old woman's cottage.

Sometimes she catches me trespassing
lures me inside with last year's chips at arm's length
until I tell her my secrets, stay and chat.

She has the features of a toad, squat, rotund,
croaky voice that misses every second or third word
white-coated tongue that darts out

over the shedding scales of skin on her lips
as she speaks. Shouts at me over the tv up too loud.
Captive, ushered into her lounge, I perch

on a sofa that matches the floral curtains. She sinks
into an arm chair that sighs in dust, her neck
puffing in and out as she breathes.

I ask the whereabouts of her teeth, she tells me
up in Annie's room behind the clock and I wonder
whether she'd mind checking there for my water pistol.

Orange Oil

at the football
my friend and I
fashion a starting line
with sticks fallen from eucalypts

take our marks
bare toes brushing bark
eyes mapping prickle patches
over our running track on the grass

as the siren sounds
we race a hundred metres
all the way back to the picnic rug
to the oily scent of sweat and oranges

her dad in shorts
grass stained whites like his
number thirty-one, throws an empty
cool drink bottle at the rubbish bin and misses

he speeds
all the way home
her mum shouting, my friend and I
sliding and grinning across the back seat

Recess in a River-town School

After spelling, the siren will sound and I will
race you to the concrete water fountains fast-
est one there gets the tap with strongest flow

then we head to the canteen crush for mock
cream buns and doughnuts filled with straw-
berry jam. I laugh at your white moustache

on a wooden bench under the veranda, legs
swinging, through plastic packets fingers rust-
ling to find the prized chip, bubble full of semi-

cooked potato. In those remaining minutes, free-
dom before reading and comprehension, we
walk, tap each pole holding up the breezeway

my other arm stretched across your shoulder
yours linked into mine, like those Italian boys
do, until a teacher urges *don't do that girls.*

Your warm breath on my ear
    she thinks we'll turn into lesbians.

The Flower Paddock

i.m. Jennette

It must have been a sense of erasure that attracted me
back to the Whadjuk ground that bordered the Canning.
I remember you cushioned deep in the grass alongside
me, smile baked on from squinting too long in the sun,
a mask of happy worn in that way we do as if conspired
wishing could alter a future, where flowers took over.

We cut off their heads, hung garlands around our necks
pondered the big questions, careful to pluck petals only
from dandelions with odd numbers, left alone all evens,
let loose their skeletons, pollen pixies to the unforseen.
As for the tiny new petals too far from maturity to count
only the calyx knew how it held back with your fate.

Problem-solving in Mathematics

I still see the face; the one with hair on the upper lip
worn to hide behind, as if to render words untraceable.

Always the same girl; black hair, dark eyes, heavy limbs,
not quite pretty, whose day you make even darker. Still

you can speak well to the blonde when she asks why
you won't stop picking on her friend, and you never do

have reason. In every class I listen to the same scenario
wishing I could speak my mind like this girl, with her.

All I have is inhibition and an idea to stab you in the eye
with a compass. So many of us and only one of you.

We just watch, when the solution is right there in the
geometry of sheer numbers and finding the right angle.

Watching the Corpse Flower

In the aftermath of lightening surge and hail, you
see a pine tree encrusted, trunk fractured, greenstick
exposed, like flesh retracted from thigh bone.
A riven vessel brings palliate glue. You watch how
amber blisters are born, adorn the scars with bling.

Trailing a rage, she crept onto me like that, her welter
all pearl and lacquer, all talc of soft ash, all
flutter and puff of white dove. So fleeting a salve
you take it in the manner it was given in that moment
one foot poised to walk away. After each deluge,

you imagine atop limestone hills, a corpse flower,
and you wait despite the miasma of rotting fish,
or a tramp's ripening socks; you wait anyway
just to witness it bloom once a year because it will
be gone again before the day's out.

The still point

i.m. Miriamme Young

comes to me in a capsule
some blend meant to calm
my name-calling voice, slapping hands
so I can no longer tell you

I barely draw breath.
They say hearing is the last sense to go
hum of a monitor
babble in the walls

the voice reciting a poem is yours
about a man who has already passed
and the grandson who notices
his light on things.

When you stop talking
the sky cracks open a little
the sun's touch feels strangely cold
makes me think of Eliot's four quartets

of *that still point in a turning world.*
I am neither here nor there,
you can believe that
the dance of this light is both moving and still.

New Beginnings

Tips of their petals shone over the mass of native donkey orchids
in the dew-soaked paddock, two fresh-trodden paths wiped bright,

leading down to the wetland bordered by tall reeds, either side
the soak wicked to thigh level on my jeans. Underbelly dripping,

the steel-grey raised her head, nickered a fog about her muzzle,
a few tiny pearls of water beaded and threaded onto whiskers.

To the right a young black thoroughbred walked in small circles
as if still in his stall at the racetrack. The old mare gave a look

as if to say *what's wrong with him?* Close up to the colt, a clue,
a patch of white hairs, their light exposed against the dark sheen

of his coat. Wiping them off and with a hold on his halter, I pushed
his rump away. He stopped circling for a moment then pulled

to regain his head. A ritual of stroking his neck, commanding him
to stand—futile, after each attempt he returned to his circle.

The mare stopped, head erect, with a wad of grass that hung still
from her mouth while she watched him saunter counter-clockwise,

then she flicked her ears, gave a full body shake from head to mane
to tail, and passed on the knowing that this was not how you did it.

She approached the black, nudged into his side until she had him pressed up flat against the fence, no longer able to circle. Stretched

tight, the steel wire squeaked. He opened and closed his mouth to her— a clack of baby talk. She let him go, lowered her head to graze.

Linger

On the tilt of my pen   you slide
onto a page etched with inklings of me, inklings of you.

A hybrid being moans in the space between words
gathering speed on its own exhalations.

The air shifts and your skirt parachutes against parchment
sending an echo shuffling towards the open door   and I turn.

I think I hear you in the creaking of floorboards, magpie lyrics,
my own voice, so you can never be gone, not now, not now

you dance atop my feet, light like the child-self,
not quite touching the ground.

Twilight

Not long until dusk when this image glows particulate. Blur
of a magpie on the front step anticipates your last crumbs,

takes fruit from your fingers and swallows it whole beneath
the Wandu, spits a grape seed at your Sunday shoes. Walking

ghost of you gathers the grain, sees it planted by the verandah.
This time capsule carries to the future your ripening fruit.

Your word he carols in the night, the long night, thirty or so earth
verses imprinted on his plumes, each feather a fully inked quill.

For a moment the mantel clock ticks backwards. In your cottage
I hear the old walnut piano playing Rachmaninoff and Bach.

I hear the copper clang in the wash house and the kettle muffle
a scream on the Metters, the bathroom door squeak as it closes.

Just on dark, I hear you brush past books in your library, reading
Hemingway out loud in the greying light, on loan a distant voice.

A Name Chiselled in the Wood

Her face fell open like the tree of the fallen
wept at the fragility of lost friends, of daffodils,
of fractious peace, of over-ripe summer fruit
spilled to earth. Her eyes and nose painted
closed but she could hear him, yes she could
hear him, his wretched pleas pitching higher
as he dwindled under the righteous voice
of the citadel, sullied and shrunken by its spit.
She brailles over his symbol for he is scarred
with the brand he shares with the tree, cut down
for growing too tall in all the wrong places.

Disequilibrium at 11 Old York Rd

Once inside the place   you notice
        there exists a tilt to the earth   faint
        aftermath of a giddy ride.
Your house slumps on its joints
        creaking in the corner the bookcase
                leans crooked against a pot plant
as an old man   having nodded off
        on a long car ride with the family
        one small grandchild   squeezed
                onto the door in the back seat.

I stand unsettled in this dim light
        check my inner ear for water or wax
        close both eyes   stand on one leg
picture myself falling onto soft grass
                having just jumped from a roundabout
                        still spinning empty in the playground.

This tangible lean to the right
        is that you with a change of mind
                an attempt to restore the balance?

Out Seeking Mimetomorphs

Photo: *Writer Katharine Susannah Prichard visits a gold mine as research for a novel*

Photographer and year unknown

The photograph is black and white, I imagine
delivered by box brownie sometime late art deco.
Despite the fading, the contrast is still there.
Looking at the scene, I half expect to hear a bush
ballad in the background or, from behind scribbly
gums, a gust of horse laughter and song.

Miners stand in the middle of a nowhere which,
on second glance, could well be the goldfields.
Men in prospecting pants and Homicide hats
dry sieve the earth for evidence of gold on a day
so pale and cloudless the sky is a blank. I try to
tell the time by the sharp shadow of things.

It's late morning or early afternoon. Must be a
thousand images like this of the Aussie bush
which, if placed side by side, could resemble
a single picture taken with a wide-angle lens.
Of course, it is the figure to the left of centre
beside the mine canopy who catches the eye.

A woman sixty-odd, floral print frock, crisp
white overcoat, hat and dress shoes stands in dirt.
At first you might think she's some poor woman
gotten off her bus at the wrong stop, or
the Queen visiting a third world. *Excuse me,*
would you gentlemen mind very much telling me the way to...

But her right hand gestures toward the camera
while the left reaches behind one of the men
in that way you do when posing for a photo
with a person of significance. Out of place she
may be, but she is the focus of attention here.
Strange that the photographer picks a moment

of capture when her face is obscured by the shade
of her wide-brim hat. Yet I can see her features
reflected in unusual places, what remains of her
smile etched in the earth, on a cloud, the bark
of a tree. The way this day is falling, light into gold
dust into shade into shadow, you could find it

possible to conjure up almost anything out there
in the waves of rippling heat. Tip of a mammoth
nugget lying just below the surface, a bubbling
billabong filling just over the rise, or whole lives
morphed from rock and the scars of eucalypts
to be transferred onto the pages of her next novel.

On the Strength of a Dark Black Coat

One day someone will make it into a film
you know the one   that way it bends your mind
you know the scenario well. A dancer doesn't make it
home one mid-winter night.   It isn't clear how she dies
found buried on a track in Kings Park   head first
arms crossed   a curious pattern around her neck
        covered with native twigs and leaves
                seed of liquidambar in her hair.

The accused wears a suit and tie   expensive shoes
works the nature of crime   (an attorney once told me
        magistrates don't control justice   lawyers do)
he monitors her telephone conversations
        likes to gamble on horses and women. News headlines
tag a demon, and it's done. His defence doesn't want your opinion.
                There will be no jury. You can't help
but wonder if he were indigenous   or a dry-eyed woman
he might be in prison by now.

But people talk   of the panic after she first went missing
        after the dance
        while she was still one of Schrödinger's cats
how he took to the stairs two at a time   and the crying
wanting to know   not where she is   but who knows
        about the breakdown of marriage   not asking
if anyone has heard from her   not letting in the police
they will find her coat on the bed
        the one she wore dancing
        the one she brought home the night she died
                the home with the liquidambar tree in the yard.

Same Formal Cause

With the streetlamp broken I lie curled,
wait for the timid touch of sleep. In the back
ground I can hear the taunts of youth and you,
you walk in my house in that way you did
so many times before. Its walls bear the chatter,

all our conversations held there, our voice print
bonded to clay. Even after five thousand years
only half will be forgotten or decayed or maybe
this house will be dismantled, all we've said
relocated brick by brick into new lives or maybe

they just crumble to earth always on the cusp
of death or reincarnation. If you held a water glass
to the wall could you hear the rattling of vowels
worked loose with mortar, releasing diphthongs
to the air as they leave through the open window.

In this room we spoke of the mundane things
pavlova and ginger wine, how eating green apples
together with hot tea simulates the sour taste
of vomit or Hershey's. In the ten years since,
my laundry wall has become a fireplace and a brick

barbecue, the occasional door stop. Much of my body
has gone, recycled to not sure where, though a voice
print remains, missing a few pieces of punctuation here
and there. When I breathe, there's the sough of ghosts
or sea. I don't know anymore what is inside or out.

Memory of Onions

Green flags of Auxonne wave
welcome on the breeze they shall
give to me their most fragrant
salutations, shed upon me in early
morning a balmy gale of onions.
Rows of bulbs baking down, hot
August dirt turns my tears acid
my voice E flat. I want to sing
crying songs in the field and fall
upon them in a swoon of winking
eyes cleansed as a raw wound
stings in the sea. Wash myself ancient
in waters of the Saone, swaddled
by the scent of my mother's hands.

Occasional False Memories of Black Monday (19th October 1987)

pillow, duvet, nap
sleep is not spoken—it's a lure word to check if you're awake

awake to error, and prediction can be just as faulty as memory recall
recall a grandmother crowned homecoming queen five decades late

late is better than never, she says, *after all it was the great depression*
depression is the stock market plummeting like a wingless plane

plane crash? She does remember something falling from the sky
sky is blue, morning is chilly, simply the start of another week

week long a man is living inside a billboard, he waves to you
you offer a *pillow* and for the homeless a donation of food

food crops are failing in Ethiopia despite all that August rain
rain won't help Moscow's potatoes, so they repurpose alcohol plants

plants' little straw skeletons stop the growth of tumour
tumour leaves a first lady, she eats papaya, her left breast missing

missing cellist Jacqueline du Pré already, she's dying today
today is still in the dark after a night of stormy weather

weather man didn't see it coming and will never live it down
down spills from my newly washed *duvet* split in two

two trains collide in Jakarta, people left clinging to platforms
platforms of oil in the Persian Gulf are set on fire by US

US number one hit song from Michael Jackson is Bad
bad planning loses our rainforest a world heritage status

status of women's legs rise with waistlines high on dresses
dresses by Lacroix are 'pretty, witty and gay' says he

he receives a pelting of carnations from the people
people super-glue themselves to a security tower in protest

protest at Pine Gap as a ten-year lease draws to a close
close weave, texture, grain, shag, warp and woof, nap

nap, yes, although I'm sure I heard *sleep* on your lips as well
well one out of four words in this poem could be misleading

The Terrible Stars

'Bundara Nganhula!' — Esther Simpson's letter to The Mulga Mail

Elders watch sky, *Yurla nyinyanyulu*, what star is coming?
Hear all big mob, five or six of them, we rolling up dinner
tiny grains, feel the tremble, sparkle hot, inside mountain
ngurlunmana frighten all of us, strange bodies trailing smoke
Yurla! Something out there, above the fencing camp it flies
bundara loud, bad light travelling toward us, run, get down!

Bundara bundara! Old fella cry and cry, star he coming
he coming at us! Run to *wiirlula*, jump inside the well
let singing begin, keep your head above the level of *baba*
not a safe place for swimming. Ah! Aunty has seen them
smoking, more of them now, from where across the sky?
She yelling what's going on? Hell of a racket, she let go

the handle and the water *baba* fall away, and aunty sings
listen how the wind he talking, *winthu wangga*, whispering
she hear that first, wind tell of one star, no many, *bundara*
coming to get us, terrible lights in the sky, time for dreaming
oh, everyone is saying it, singing out what this world doing?
Nhaala yanajimanha? Nhaala yanajimanha? The horses

wanna gallop home, hysterical. A family waiting at camp
old people eating in bough sheds, laying down *tharndi-*
tharndingga, listening to it roar, hands over eyes, shelter
of sapling and spinifex. *Walybala* smoking in homestead
we shout *bundara nganhula*, the star is coming, now we
wanna roll up dinner, wanna go to the well, wanna see

Maaja boss, he tell us *walybala* Englishmen going north
bomb a place up there, Montebello, we don't remember
what year it was, *Ugarla yalyba*, long time ago, overhead
jets they smoking, off to see them blow up the island
marlbagardi ngathala , terrible stars dropping down to die
turn on the wireless, listen to the news. Under our shell

we wired, forever watch for smoke since long time, run
to *baba*, safe at the waterhole, lot of funny thing happen
on this day, *bundara* falling from sky, old wind talking.

Trimouille

I
      sounds like tremor or tremble
from an island that will come to imitate its sound
pearl fishers gather to haul in the morning
catch   sailors drift to shore on a frigate
      like seabirds heavy with brood looking for a safe place to nest.
Moments after the shell is cracked   mud and water
      spiral to a silt of lime and fishes.

Close enough to hear the countdown backs turn to the bay
      faces fettered by hands   when blue
lightning breaks the barrier of skin and flesh
exposes the pattern of knuckle and bone. Hands
tighten over the eyes of ordinary men when they know
      the power of superheroes—
they must be thinking they could fly.

Picture a row of skindivers   deep underwater
caught first in a pressure wave   then a suction wave
whole bodies billowing   like balloons
*   the unseen dance of hot wind suddenly visible.*

After mushroom cloud creeps across the Pilbara sky
hundreds of thousands of turtles come
     to lay dead with the fish   on the beach
where the oystercatchers drop from flight.

There's a scar in the near shallows
      three hundred metres wide and six metres deep
and from the crater   fragments of the burning ship
        fling across two borders.

II
Falling out of the day
two guys shake seawater from sun-bleached hair
     sit back   read about it in the Sunday Times
        how not to   disturb soil   touch relics.

        They man the radio station on the island
send signals to passing ships on the trail of gas
and in between
     swim with dolphins in the lagoon
        throw a line to the coral reef
           barbecue emperor and cod
              while dugong forage in seagrass
camp   a short walk from ground zero.

Metal and debris?   oh stacks of it
    stumble over it all the time
        use it to hold down the flaps on the tent
          mate.

Radio activity   sounds like operating the wireless.

Twice I Peeked at a Blinding Star

Being military
you weren't as defiant as I
would have been—or maybe
I wouldn't. It's difficult to know
when the gullibility of faith
or the ignorance of trust
could fling me backward
like a dangerous religion.

At first you thought the sound
wasn't coming, that implosion
meant everything happened
on the inside, like worry
in some solitary hour of night.

And in those few silent seconds
beyond the call of zero
the intense light gave away
nothing. But even fireworks
can bring an aftershock
and no matter how hard you try
you jump but can't look away
as light fades to dust and ash.

I know the awe in that
soundless moment like when
the moon passes over the sun
and the dampening of fear
that comes with sudden dark.

The Pact of Forgetting

Autumn Cannibalism, Salvador Dali, 1936-7

An apple of liberty sits on too many heads,
its core a ring of bullets, you will make
their deaths seem like an inner bleed

Barcelona will never forget

This new civilscape comes near to ground,
I fall into you, you into me, a blanket
of quick lime speeds the decay

Dali will never forget

See how my winter melons flow,
measure intimacy by the depth of a spoon,
the ripe of rind, the strength of bread-lace

Mujeres Libres will never forget

Our skins are liquid in the sun
no longer the barrier they once were
my aorta grows a branch in your sleeve

Roots of olive trees will never forget

The rose of fire wears a faded banner
on the brick wall outside, she is the old
keeper of the books that won't be denied

Street names will never forget

Once I heard that the pact was broken
I became much more talkative than you
and a little hungry

Similitude

...he thinks not only with his brain, with his knitted brow, his distended nostrils and compressed lips, but with every muscle of his arms, back, and legs, with his clenched fist and gripping toes.
Rodin

You declare this night as beyond remedy, lie
        supine on its damp cotton, let the storm
of me settle over you, our argument forced
        deep in the pocket of your open mouth.

To my sleepy eye, you seem to consume
        the dark, as if it weren't too large to swallow,
and I can only think of how it might lodge
        in your throat, choke you upon waking.

Once dream comes for you, you don't go
        willingly. You flip onto hands and knees,
forehead heavy on the pillow, fist against
        your teeth, like a woman bearing down.

But lighting changes everything. Tonight
        with Mars on the rise, your skin flushes
incandescent bronze, and I imagine you to be
        Rodin's *Thinker* tipped forward as if dead

tired, exhausted by all those mercurial lyrics
        and unsolved equations in your head, leaving
you ungrounded. You are your own radical
        Cleveland bomber attempting to stop a fight

while I'm next to you trying to understand
        the conversation of your fingers arching
and flexing, pointing and relaxing, scratching
        at the space where your feet used to be.

Mouth to Mouth

My forefinger strokes your sleek blue snake
vein pulsing purple at each touch of skin on skin
my bones pummel a cut-time rhythm on your chest
a sharp taste of metal on your fervoured tongue

Your vein pulsing purple at each touch of skin on skin
shudder of breath tinged with the quick ice of mint
a sharp taste of metal on your fervoured tongue
you don't see your pupils shrink to the point of a pin

Shudder of breath tinged with the quick ice of mint
falls as still as fear against my cheek but you don't notice
you don't see your pupils shrink to the point of a pin
your lashes flutter shut and your lips fade to pale

As still as fear against my cheek, you don't notice
you don't feel me landing astride your hip bones
your lashes flutter shut and your lips fade to pale
nor hear me screaming at the telephone for an ambulance

You don't feel me landing astride your hip bones
pummel a cut-time rhythm on your chest with my fist
or hear me screaming at the telephone for an ambulance
forefinger pressed against your sleek blue snake

The Last Bath

Fleur du sel dans ma belle baignoire
      toes clawed against the cold tiles
from the tap   tepid water brings the sea.

Water yields to swallow me whole
lapping against skin   visceral
      as two lovers separated by glass.

I sink beneath the meniscus   beneath your hand
my fingers enmeshed in your curls   dragging
      the hound is in your face.

It occurs to me the first one to drown
      will be unable to finish the other.
To be both killer and killed yet so unequal in death.

After the Late Night Joys

after Paddy Green, my fourth great grandfather, Evans Music Hall,
Covent Garden, 1856

Soft thud of a snuff box closing, and the glitter
of stray motes. *We're dust of quite another sort*

here, around the glow from the bare bulb head-
high on the night stand. Their energy is haloed

around the ghost light left lit at front of stage.
You can hear all those voices thrown from walls.

Shadows are heavy with them. A bold nakedness
about lyrics sung without the company of music

or audience. Paddy paused, nodding. They'd say
he was playing to the haircuts, lecturing the skull.

He squatted on the edge of the stage, pondering
whether or not an actor's spirit could be inhaled.

'We're dust of quite another sort here' (Fay Zwicky, from 'Isfahan' in New Poems)

Acknowledgements

An earlier version of this manuscript was shortlisted for *The Noel Rowe Poetry Award 2017*
My gratitude to Philip Neilsen for his mentorship and helpful critique on the final stages of this manuscript on behalf of The Queensland Poetry Festival's Emerging Older Poet Mentorship Award 2018

Several poems were first published as follows:
'Patternicity', *Overland* 232, October 2018; 'In the theatre of time-on-sky', 'Someone's Lost Sock' and 'Close to Flying', Overland Online, August 2018; 'Flare-ups and Diminishings' and 'Foal Watch', *Southerly* 77:3, 2018; 'After the Late Night Joys', *Westerly*, 63:1, 2018; 'Alligatorwood', *Westerly* 62:2, 2017; 'Chasing Cello Joe', *Meanjin*, Autumn 2017; 'Unpicking a Bird', *Cordite Poetry Review* 81: Land, 2017; 'The Fetishist Listener', *Poetry d'Amour*, 2017; 'Juniper', *Lane Cove Literary Awards 2016: An Anthology*, May 2017; 'Me, Susan & Jacques Prévert', *The Henry Kendall Poetry Awards Anthology*, October 2017; 'Linger', *Australian Love Poems*, 2013; 'Neruda's Sixteen Finches', *Cordite Poetry Review* 49: Obsolete, February 2015; 'Nude Descending a Staircase', *Cuttlefish* 01, 2015; *Award Winning Australian Writing*, 2015; 'Like the Finch', *Poetry d'Amour*, 2015; 'The Light Painter' and 'Mouth to Mouth', *Regime* 05, 2015; 'a day breaks in two rocks', *Westerly* 59:2, 2014; 'Harlequin Street', *Award Winning Australian Writing*, 2014; 'Plume', *Trove* vol. 2 no.1, April 2011

Several poems in this collection have been reproduced from my 2016 chapbook *Aporiac* with permission from Finishing Line Press, Kentucky, USA.

The following poems received acknowledgement in various competitions:
'In the theatre of time-on-sky' was Highly Commended in the *Ros Spencer Poetry Contest* 2018;
'Patternicity' was Commended in *The Ros Spencer Poetry Contest* 2018;
'Last Words' was Commended in the *PCWC Patrons Poetry Awards* 2018;
'The Sleepover Sonnets' was longlisted in the *Fish Flash Fiction Contest* 2018;

'Foal Watch' received a Highly Commended award in the *PCWC Patron's Prize* 2017;

'With a Naked Eye' received a Highly Commended award in the *PCWC Patron's Prize* 2017;

'Me, Susan & Jacques Prévert' was shortlisted for the *Henry Kendall Poetry Prize* 2017;

'Unpicking a Bird' received second place in the *Glen Phillips Poetry Competition* 2016;

'Chasing Cello Joe' received a Commended award in the *PCWC Patron's Prize* 2016;

'A Geranium Grows in the Wall' was Commended in the *PCWC Patron's Prize* 2016;

'Juniper' was shortlisted for *The Lane Cove Literary Award* 2016;

'The Fetishist Listener' was longlisted for *The Adrien Abbott Prize* 2016;

'Transience' was selected for the *AGWA 'Verse for Art'*, August 2016;

'Twilight' received 3rd place in the *OOTA Spilt Ink Competition* 2014;

'Nude Descending a Staircase' won first place in the *KW Treanor Poetry Comp* 2014;

'Sometimes behind the Wallpaper' received second place in *The KJ Bates Poetry Comp* 2014;

'Woman in the Waters of Lethe' was Commended in the *OOTA Spilt Ink Poetry Comp* 2014;

'Harlequin Street' won first place in the *KW Treanor Poetry Comp* 2013.